Dropshipping:

The Ultimate Beginners' Guide to Dropshipping Success.

By: David Jackson

Table of Conten

Description

I want to thank you and congratulate you for downloading the book, " Dropshipping: The Ultimate Beginner's Guide to Drop Shipping Success."

This book contains proven steps and strategies on how to successfully run and succeed in a dropshipping. This book will not only guide you through the dropshipping process, but it will also help you when deciding on the products to sell and picking the right supplier. Aside from that, the book also includes tips on how to minimize your expenses while maximizing on the income.

Grab your copy today and get started in your journey to success!

Best of Luck!

Introduction

What is Dropshipping?

When you do online shopping, there's a big chance that you have already encountered dropshipping. The reason is that most of the stores that you see online do not keep their items on their stockroom – instead, they get the items that their customers order from another store and then ship them directly to their customers. That means that the owners of these online stores probably never had to handle or see the products that they sell.

Dropshipping VS Retail Stores

For many people who have done dropshipping and made a killing out of it, this business model saved them from spending too much capital just to run their own business. Here are some reasons why you may want to do dropshipping instead of keeping a brick-and-mortar shop:

1. You don't need much capital.

This is arguably the biggest advantage that the dropshipping business model can offer. Since you do not have to invest thousands of dollars to keep an inventory, you can keep your online store without having to worry about how you are going to keep stock of the products that you offer your customers. Also, since there is no need to stock your items, you do not have to spend for a warehouse.

It also follows that you do not need to have a lot of money in order to get started in the business. As long as you know where you can source the products that you are offering and fulfill orders placed by your customers, you can keep the ball running.

2. You don't have to worry much about the overhead.

Many of the most successful dropshipping businesses are run through a computer in a home office, with an overhead of $100 or less. While these expenses are likely to grow as you expand your business, the overhead that you need to maintain is still lower compared to having an actual retail store.

3. You can work anywhere.

You can run a dropshipping business anywhere in the world as long as you have an internet connection. Since you are not tied down to a physical store, you can move to a location where the cost of living is much lower to further lower your overhead costs.

4. Enjoy unlimited product selection.

Since you do not have to pre-purchase any item that you want to sell, you do not have to worry about limitations in items that you can sell. If you can find a supplier for any item that you have in mind, you can list that item for sale on your dropshipping site without having to pay for the item in advance.

5. Dropshipping is scalable.

When you open a retail shop, the amount of profit that you enjoy is directly proportional to the amount of work that you put in. That means that if you want to increase your profit to 300%, you have to work three times harder.

Dropshipping, on the other hand, entails that your suppliers will be doing most of the work. You can always get additional orders by leveraging suppliers, allowing your business to grow without having to do too much additional work.

Now that you know the perks that you can get out of this business, it's time to get started!

Chapter 1 Understanding The Basics Of Dropshipping

To venture into any field and do anything well, it is best to first understand the venture. This is why understanding dropshipping and its benefits is imperative. Let us look at what dropshipping basically is and why this fulfillment model is incredibly lucrative and feasible for you.

Dropshipping: What It Is And How It Works

Dropshipping is a simple retail fulfillment approach wherein you don't have to stock the products you sell. It is quite different from the traditional retail fulfillment approach wherein the storeowner has to maintain stock of goods it deals in. On the contrary, when you start a dropshipping business, you don't have to worry about stocking the goods you sell at all.

Instead, you choose the products you want to deal in from the supplier, who serves as the third party in this case and the third party delivers the ordered items to your customers once orders have been placed.

To start a dropshipping business, first, you have to locate one or more drop shipping suppliers depending on what you want to sell. Next you enter a contract with the supplier upon payment of a fee charged by the supplier. The supplier then provides you with product images, description, and other details that you display on your website or social media account or any platform that you use to market and sell your goods. You obviously have the option of marketing your business using any method you find appropriate.

Once a customer places an order, you get their details such as name, shipment address, email address, and other details (mostly required and mentioned by the supplier) and send them to the dropshipping wholesaler. Mostly, wholesalers demand you get the payment from the customer in advance so your customers will be required to have a debit card to make the payment. However, COD (cash on delivery) service is available nowadays too and is becoming more popular with time.

As soon as the wholesaler gets the information you sent them, they start to process the respective order, which usually takes 7- 10 business days and at times 2 weeks. The order is then directly shipped to the customer who placed the order. You never even see let alone receive the product or stock it and just have to serve as the middleperson between the wholesaler and the customer.

Using this approach, you make money by getting products on wholesale rates from the supplier and then selling them at retailer rates to the customers. The profit margin varies from one product to another, but generally, appliances and electronics are considered well-paying goods in this business.

With only a few hundred dollars and the will to move forward, you can start your very own dropshipping business and turn it into a successful venture. Now let us look at why this business model is incredibly lucrative.

Chapter 2 Benefits of Dropshipping

Dropshipping is a fast-growing industry because of its many benefits. Here are a few examples:

1. Less Capital

Dropshipping companies have no need to handle and store inventory for their business. Hence, there is no need for a huge amount of capital. This is the biggest advantage of this kind of business model because it does not require the outflow of money just to buy inventory.

Traditionally, business owners need to spend thousands of dollars on inventory prior to jump-starting their business. With dropshipping, these business owners can put their money into something else aside from inventory like the development of a professional website.

2. Purchase upon making a sale

With dropshipping, merchants will only need to purchase their inventory whenever they make a sale to their customers. This means that a business owner does not even have to spend his own money to buy inventory. It is actually possible to put up this business with very little amount of money because the customers will technically be the one paying for the inventory from the suppliers.

3. Easy to Start

Anyone can start a dropshipping company even in the comforts of their home. Aside from the very small amount of money needed to put up a dropshipping business, this business model is easy to start. All you have to do is find a reliable supplier with a great product that can be sold to the market. The key here is to know who to make business with and what products to sell.

4. Low Business Risk

There is significantly lower business risk when putting up a dropshipping company. Since there is no need to spend thousands of dollars into inventory, you will not be stuck with loads of unsold inventory in case the business does not succeed.

Have you ever watched the Pursuit to Happiness? Will Smith's character was very optimistic about his new business venture. However, since his product was not in demand in the medical industry, he had trouble selling it. Aside from that, he bought the entire inventory beforehand. So, when he could not sell his goods, he ran out of available money that could have been used for other essentials. With dropshipping, you will not have to worry about getting into a situation similar to that of Will Smith's character in the movie.

5. Low Overhead

Aside from low capital requirement, you will no longer need to spend much on overhead because you will not need to manage loads of inventory. In fact, a huge number of dropshipping companies are actually managed by owners through their homes with only a laptop. Dropshippers that work from home end up spending just roughly $100 a month on overhead.

Obviously, the amount of overhead will eventually grow as your company grows but this is relatively lower compared to other brick and mortar or traditional business models.

6. Wide Array of Products

The sky is the limit in terms of what you want to sell in your dropshipping business. You can actually sell a wide variety of products because you do not have to pre-purchase all of them for resale. As long as your supplier has a particular item in stock, you can also list that up in your inventory for your customers. In a sense, you are just going to be a very effective intermediary for the supplier.

7. Flexible Area Location

As long as you have internet connection, you can put up your own dropshipping company anywhere you want to. You can even just setup your laptop next to your bed and start this business without changing out of your pajamas. As long as you find reliable suppliers and you can communicate with customers easily, you can successfully manage this type of business.

8. Easy Work Scale

With dropshipping, business owners can easily scale their workload because most of the leveraging will be done by the dropshipping suppliers. You will only need to take in customer orders and suppliers will bear all the additional processes needed to fulfill that particular order. Hence, you can actually expand your business with very little incremental work.

In cases of customer dispute, you will definitely have to put more work that is related with customer service. However, you have to keep in mind that this kind of problems can be avoided if you personally know your suppliers as well as the quality of products that they can put out.

These are only a few of the most common reasons why this type of business model is growing. All of these benefits make dropshipping very attractive to businesspersons. However, this does not mean that dropshipping does not come with a price.

Chapter 3 Disadvantages of Dropshipping

In the previous chapter, we talked about the many benefits of dropshipping. To give readers an unbiased view of dropshipping, here are some of its disadvantages:

1. Low Profit

Given the fact that business owners do not have a need to put in a large capital investment, this type of business also does not give out a huge amount of profits. There is a low margin of profit in this type of business because of the highly competitive niche. There are loads of merchants offering the same types of products at varied prices.

Since it is very easy to put up, most merchants can actually start up their websites with very little investment and offer their products at very low prices as an attempt to lure in customers.

Given the very low prices offered by other websites, most dropshipping businesspersons find it necessary to lower their prices in order to compete. Customers will always find it a need to find products at lower prices. No matter how up to date and nice your website is, they will always end up comparing products by price even if your competition has a very low-quality website.

2. Issues on Inventory

As stated in the previous chapter, dropshipping companies do not usually handle their merchandise personally. All the handling and shipping process will be the supplier's job. Hence, the dropshipping company does not have physical inventory of the product. Some products may be of low quality without the dropshipping company's knowledge.

Suppliers can easily give the dropshipping company high-end products as samples but ship low quality rip-offs to customers instead. If this is the case, a dropshipping company can lose reputation from paying customers due to issues on inventory.

3. Inventory Availability

Again, suppliers are the ones carrying inventory. Hence, dropshipping companies do not always have a complete picture of the availability of products because not all suppliers have the technology to keep track of inventory.

Traditional businesses stock their own items. This makes it relatively simple to keep track of what is in stock and what is not. If a particular item is out of stock, a traditional business can easily solve it by ordering more. In case of a dropshipping company, they have no way to easily keep track of inventory because they are sourcing it from multiple suppliers. Inventory can change on a daily basis when it comes to this kind of business. Therefore, it is very important to have a good relationship with the supplier.

4. Shipping Complications

When you put up a dropshipping company, you can end up with a customer that orders products that need to be shipped by different suppliers. This kind of transaction can actually complicate your computation for shipping costs.

This is especially true if your suppliers are from different locations that involve different shipping costs. If this kind of transaction happens, you have to find a way to keep customers from thinking that you are grossly overcharging them for shipping.

5. Errors of the Supplier

It is also possible to get problems with customers due to errors by the supplier. Even though this seems like a case of being blamed for someone else's fault, dropshipping companies should accept the responsibility in dealing with this kind of problems.

Dropshipping companies are responsible for these mistakes because customers bought from their company and have no idea as to where the product is actually shipped. In the end, the customer trusted your company for high quality products and not the supplier.

Is it Worth the Trouble?

Dropshipping, as with traditional businesses, is not a perfect business model. This is not a stress-free type of business that can provide owners with easy money. Even though this business model has numerous advantages, it also comes with many risks.

Just like anything in this world that is actually worth anything, you will have to work with what you have in order to make the most in this kind of business. Do not fret because this book aims to help you in that process.

Chapter 4 Top Tips for Becoming a Successful Dropshipping Genius

Planning and knowing the pitfalls are excellent steps towards becoming a successful dropshipper; they will certainly reduce your chances of failure in what is a very competitive market. However, to really make the most of this business opportunity you need to go a stage further and proactively focus on developing and building your business. The following tips will help to ensure you become a dropshipping genius:

Seasonal Products

You should be aware, well in advance of the seasonal variations. As a wholesaler you should be stocking Ester products as soon as Christmas is finished; or summer products as soon as Easter is done. Seasonal products are extremely popular and can be very lucrative; providing you plan ahead and are ready for the demand. One particular benefit of a seasonal product is that they are generally bought every year; people will buy the same thing as the year before because they have chucked it at the end of the season or lost it.

You will also find that much of the seasonal items are not available in your average retail store. They simply cannot afford to take the risk that they will be stuck with a range of seasonal products that cannot be sold and must be stored or thrown. This reduces the level of competition and makes it easier for you to capitalize on the demand.

You may find it easier to set up a calendar which reminds you which stock you should be buying when; so that you are never caught out.

Product Bundles

This is an excellent way to sell additional products. Instead of one customer buying one item, they will buy three, knowing that the third item is free or heavily reduced. The result for you is additional turnover and profit, provided you pay attention when you set the price. You will also receive good feedback from the customer as they tell their friends about the offer; your business should increase!

Another advantage of bundling products is that you can reduce the associated shipping charge and you can add a higher profit margin item to a lower profit margin item which sells exceptionally well. This will improve your profit margin on the low margin item whilst giving the customer a good deal; this will also ensure they return and become a repeat customer.

Sell Products you Know

It is especially important when you are first starting out to sell only products you know. For your social media postings and your website content you need to be able to write informative content; something which will establish that you know your market and your product and allow others to respect you. This respect and trust will lead to them buying from you, even if you are not the cheapest. If you wish to add products in to your range in the future which you do not know so much about it is advisable to do a little research; ideally purchase one which can be used yourself to ensure you fully understand its uses and functionality.

It is particularly important that you never promote a product that you do not know and fully endorse. If you something is good and that you would use it to encourage sells people who respect you are likely to buy it. If the product then turns out to be rubbish, your credibility and reputation will be gone in moments; it can be very difficult to regain a reputation when you have destroyed it.

Niche Products

The best products to attempt to find are those which are in a niche. The market is much less likely to be saturated with these types of products and you will be able to enjoy higher profit margins and probably a smaller range of products. Your marketing will also be easier as you will know exactly what kind of people buy the product. Yu can then set your campaign to deal directly with them and appeal to them.

It is very important to know your product inside out if you are dealing with a niche market. Reputation is doubly important in this type of scenario and you will probably be dealing with people who know a significant amount about a certain product. Knowing your product means you can provide excellent customer service and build your customer base through satisfied customers, with minimal effort.

However, it is important to remember that the potential customer base is smaller for a niche market and your reputation can be destroyed quicker than with a more mainstream product. As such you should encourage communication with your customers and experts in the field; the knowledge shared can benefit everyone in the community.

Different Markets

It can be very tempting to start out by targeting EBay or Amazon; however, there are lots of different market places and it is important to be present in as many of them as possible. The more markets you are active in the easier it will be to find customers; this is simply a numbers game!

Not only will selling in different markets enable you to reach customers that you might not otherwise see, it will also enable you to play with the prices of the products and establish what to charge where. You may found that people on certain marketplaces are willing to pay more than those in others; this is simply a case of expectations. A good business person will happily cater for these needs and charge a higher price where appropriate; you can always offer to price match if this helps to get the sale!

It is important to look at each type of market to establish the type of customer who tends to shop their; this may affect the way you market the product. Never be afraid to try different approaches until you find the one that works!

Shipping rates

Research indicates that people are more likely to purchase from you if you offer free shipping. This does not mean that you cannot charge shipping! The best approach to shipping costs is to add them into the sales price; your customer will believe they are getting free shipping when in fact they are paying for it. If you can get free shipping from your dropshipper then you will be able to improve your profit margins.

It is also worth looking at what effect the shipping costs can have on a bundle. Again, build the cost of the shipping into your sales figure; but be sure to emphasis to your customer that they will get free shipping if they buy three products or more. You will be surprised at how often people will go for the deal as they perceive they are getting something for nothing. In fact studies show that if someone is offered free shipping they are more likely to purchase multiple products from a supplier.

Customer Service – Reputation

This is an essential part of becoming a successful business and in the modern age is something that must be worked on constantly. A reputation can take a long time to establish and build; it can be destroyed in a matter of moments with a bad reaction which is blown out of proportion on a social media site.

To ensure this is not an issue you need to seize every opportunity to interact with your customers. A query should be responded to quickly and a complaint dealt with fairly. The faster your response the more trust you will establish with your customers and this will ensure you gain repeat business and personal recommendations. This is the best way to grow your business! There may be times when it seems impossible to reach an agreement with a customer; the best approach in this situation is usually to refund them and allow them to keep the product or to replace it free of charge with a better one. There will be a cost involved which must be absorbed by you. However, this can be compensated for by turning potentially damaging publicity into an acknowledgment of how good your customer service is.

Ready For Change

No matter how good your plan or your strategy there will be opportunities that arise and issues that have not been foreseen. You must be ready for these and able to evaluate them according to the information you have on the current market and your customers. It is natural for any business to evolve and change; in fact it is essential for a business to survive. Knowing your product, your market and even the larger economy will allow you to react, develop and expand according to the opportunities that present themselves to you.

There will be issues and even bad decisions along the way; it is impossible to build a business without making some mistakes. The real trick is to learn from the mistakes and be prepared to change direction as soon as you realise that a specific strategy is not working.

Expansion

To become a successful dropshipping business you will need to expand. You can choose to expand by increasing your range of products or by expanded into a different market sector. It is even possible to do both options! When expanding you will need to evaluate the market you are expanding into and ensure that there is both demand for your new product and that the market is not already saturated. Dropshipping makes it very easy for you to test new products on your existing customer base as you do not have a cash outlay; you can simply add the product and see what happens. It is easy to stop selling a product and try something different if it is not favourably received.

The process you go through will actually help your dropship supplier as well as they can see which products are selling and which are not. The key to successful expansion is to take the process slowly, introduce a small number of new products at a time; evaluate and correct your choices if necessary before bringing in the next new batch.

Staffing

Starting in dropshipping is relatively easy and certainly affordable. However, as your business grows you will eventually need someone else to assist you in running the business. Social media and customer service, in particular, can consume a huge amount of your energy and time. This time and energy could be better spent improving your product and expanding your business.

When you need to look at the bigger picture and focus on where your business is going, you will need to take on a reliable assistant; ideally they should have a good manner, as much of what they will be doing is dealing with customers to promote the business profile. Choose your assistant carefully, even if this means upsetting family members;

the right person will help to build your company, the wrong one can quickly ruin your hard work.

Campaigns & Social Media Tracking

To expand your business, you will need to ensure your existing customer base is aware of your new product range and that you can attract a new group of customers. This can be achieved by email marketing, blogs and weekly newsletters to your customer base. You can also make posts on your website and social media accounts which will build the excitement of a new product and get people interested in what you are offering.

Once you have a campaign running you will need to use one of the many software apps available to track the visitor numbers to your website, the number of 'bounces' (people who arrive at your site and leave again), and the number of people who convert to customers once they have visited your site. This information is essential for understanding the effect and response of any campaign. Once you know which campaigns and approaches work you will be able to build on these and drop the other methods. This will enable your customer base to grow steadily as you expand your stock and market share.

Real Stock

Dropshipping does not need to be the end result; it can become part of a business. Although holding stock means incurring storage costs and having the risk of capital outlay which cannot be released; it can also offer the opportunity to increase your profit dramatically. Wholesalers will be happy to offer a discounted rate if you are buying a product from them in bulk; this is not something they can afford to do of you are buying one product at a time via dropshipping. Buying the product in bulk at a cheaper price gives you the option of selling at the same price and making additional money or selling at your current profit margin and increasing your appeal in the marketplace as one of the cheapest suppliers. You can even use a very popular product as a loss leader; sell it for a loss as it will bring customers in and they will purchase other items.

There are logistical issues and more risk associated with holding your own stock and you may need to physically post items. However, it also has the potential to increase your profit; only you can decide which approach you prefer to take!

Chapter 5 What Products to Sell?

Now that you have set up your business and your finances are in check, you are now ready to get your e-commerce business up and running. However, this is the most important question that you need to answer before you can earn: What should you sell?

One of the most common beginner's mistakes in dropshipping is choosing a product out of personal interest. While it is a good thing that you are passionate about what you are selling, it does not mean that other people will love your product listing as much as you do. For this reason, it is better to choose a product that you can market instead.

Characteristics of a Great Dropshipping Site

A great e-commerce site is a site that customers love going to because it provides everything that they need. Customer service aside, here are the top three reasons why customers will love your site:

1. You can distribute exclusively or can offer special discounts

If it is possible for you to carry a product from a manufacturer that you can offer at a special discounted pricing or is available only through your store, then you can sell a product and make a profit out of it. However, these arrangements through suppliers are difficult to make.

2. You can offer competitive rates

Products that are such a steal are guaranteed to get a lot of attention. However, take note that other more established dropshippers can do better at a price war – trying to compete with Amazon and other large e-commerce sites by lowering your prices may strip away all your profit.

3. You offer non-pricing added value

One of the best ways to sell your product is to offer information about it. This does not only tell your customers that they need your product in their lives, but also sets you apart from other dropshippers. By offering your customers the information that they need about all the products that you sell, you establish yourself as an expert in a niche, which makes you stand out as the best shop to buy from.

What is the Best Product to Sell?

If you want to get special attention in the market and ensure that your customers will go back to your website with another order, here are some tips that you could use when it comes to choosing products to offer:

1. Get products that have multiple components

When you offer a product that needs a lot of parts to function well, you are hitting the market of consumers that are likely to turn to the internet for assistance. When you offer products that have multiple parts, you are creating better opportunity for your business to add more value to every visit or purchase.

2. Choose products that can be customizable.

Customizable products offer plenty of opportunities for you to add value by offering guides on how customers can select the right type of products for their needs. For example, different players need different types of guitar cables, depending on their budget, performance, or gear. They may also need other types of cables to patch their pedal boards together to a single electricity source. If you can offer all their cable needs and assist them on which one they should purchase, then they do not need to find another site to place their orders on.

3. Offer products that require technical installation or setup

If you have knowledge on the products that you are offering, then it would be easy for you to offer technical support on how users can assemble their purchased products for first time use. If you can throw in a manual that includes common troubleshooting techniques, then customers will flock into your website even if the products they wanted to buy is offered somewhere for a lower price.

4. Easy to ship

In the world of dropshipping, you need to make sure that the products that you offer is not too cumbersome, easily damaged, or difficult to pack. The reason is that you are likely to incur higher shipping charges from your supplier and also increase the risk of customer returns due to damage. Unless you are confident that you will meet a supplier that can deliver orders with minimum risks, you are better off with small products that are not likely to fall apart during shipping.

5. Difficult to obtain

Products that are hard to find in malls or any local shop are the best products to sell through dropshipping. The reason for that is that these products allow you to create better profit margin and your customers would always be willing to wait until these items are delivered to them. The rarer it is for your customers, the more they would be forgiving when it comes to stock availability and shipping times.

Chapter 6 Common Problems Experienced with Drop Shipping

You have to understand that even with all of the things that are mentioned above, drop shipping is not easy. It is not exactly one of the things that you can do if you want to make a lot of money at the soonest possible time. The things that will be discussed below are common issues that you have to consider before you start the company but don't worry. As long as you are determined and as long as you know how to plan appropriately, these problems can be resolved easily.

1.   Out of stock items when customers want the same product.

The best solution to this is to make sure that you will be working with more than one supplier that can offer similar products. It is likely that some of these products are so similar that people will not notice that they are different from one another.

2.   Syncing products can be tedious and will take time.

Since you do not have all day to just properly synchronize your database about all of the products that you are offering to clients, the best solution is to have the right application or software that can do the synchronization for you. You can simply add or remove items depending on whether you would like to sell them or not.

3.   You will be selling items that you will never see.

It is true that as a drop shipper, the items that you are selling to customers are items that you will never see in person. This means that it will be harder to know if the item is really worth it or not. You can just base it on the pictures which you know, may not be too accurate.

In order to solve this problem, you can always call the supplier that you are going to get the products from to ask some questions about the product in general. In case this is not enough, why not purchase some of your most popular products and get to know their different features. You may understand why they are so popular and why you always run out of these items.

4.   You cannot control customer service.

Aside from the reputation of your company, another thing that is important is the customer service that you can provide. As a drop shipping company, you have no control over the type of service that your customers will get.

The perfect solution to this is to try your best to choose the right people who will help you and your business thrive well in this type of industry. If you feel that the people you are currently working with are doing nothing to help you give the customer service that your customers deserve, search for other people to partner with.

The Problems Your Customers Would Like to Avoid

A lot of customers know that purchasing from a drop shipping company is a great way for customers to get to see different products without having to go from one website to another. Customers know that there are also some cons when it comes to dropping shipping and they would like to avoid it. Here are a few common problems and how you can make sure that your customers will not experience those problems.

1.   Poor Details Regarding Orders

Whenever customers order from your drop shipping company, they would like to make sure that they will get their products immediately. In order not to disappoint your customers regarding their orders, you can send them their tracking number so that they can check the status of their orders from your website. Of course, in order to sync all of the orders, make sure that you will talk with your suppliers regarding when the items will be shipped. It will also help if you can contact the customers regarding their orders and be specific about when their orders are expected to arrive.

2.   Their Orders are not what They Expected

As an owner of a drop shipping company, you have never seen in person most of the items that you are selling. You can only base the items from the description that the suppliers give. This is the reason why there are some customers who may complain about the appearance of the items that they have received. The best thing that you can do about this is to double check the products that you are going to offer on your website ahead of time. You can contact the supplier and do not hesitate to ask questions, so you will have a clear view of the items before you let them become available through your website.

3.   The items they will get are damaged.

It can be very frustrating for a customer to get damaged items because the main reason why they have purchased from your company is so they can avoid rushing with the crowd. In case the item that gets shipped to the customer is damaged, you can please your customer by replacing the item without having to let the customer send back the damaged item. This action can win a lot of points for your drop shipping company.

Chapter 7 How to Compete with Other Dropshipping Companies

One of the problems that you are going to have when you start your own drop shipping company is the fact that you have to compete with a lot of other drop shipping companies that may be located in the same area. If you have too much competition from where you are located, it will be harder for you to be noticed especially if your competitors are already well known and have already established their reputation.

You can always opt to rely on free traffic. You would rely on how well your website has been created so that people can visit your site whenever they try to search for the use of a search engine. Yet, this can still be complicated. In order to stand out, you need to generate a good amount of traffic, and you can do this by using paid advertising.

You have to rely on your website in order to be noticed heavily and for people to come back and check the items that you are offering. Let us focus first on your website's content. Here are just some of the things that you can add:

● Consider the number of linking domains - The more links that you will have on your website, the better your website's ranking is going to be. Remember that duplicate links will not be considered by search engine sites, so they will not be effective at all.

● Consider the quality of your website. It does not mean that just because you have a lot of links, your website will already be one of the websites that will rank high in search engine sites. The quality of your content and how relevant the content will be will make a huge difference. You can compare the current quality of your website with the others with the use of different applications. Your page rank can be easily checked when you have the right tools, but in case you would like to check manually, this is possible as well.

It is evident that if you would be one of the first few websites that will appear in search engine sites; you will be checked out by more people. In case you do not understand the page ranking, here is a guide that will let you understand the differences of each:

Page Rank 1 - 2: You have a small amount of authority. This means that you are able to reach a small amount of your target market.

Page Rank 3- 4: This is the common page rank of websites that are competing well with other websites. If you get this page rank, this means that you have a high sense of authority and will be displayed in one of the first few pages of search engine sites.

Page Rank 4- 5: There are some websites who do not get to this point anymore because the website needs to be connected to other websites that are also considered to have high page ranks. To reach this rank, you need your website to be linked to different websites.

Page Rank 6+: It will be hard to compete in this type of page rank. You need to employ a full time SEO expert that will be able to let your website keep up with the changing times. At the same time, you need to make sure that your marketing is always in full gear. If you do not have professionals working for you, you will be lost in this type of page rank.

Chapter 8 Deciphering Your Page Results

Do you realize that the page results that you get are different from other people in different countries who are searching for the same things that you have typed in the search bar? This is because search engine sites make it a point to consider your geographic location. This makes searching for the right items to sell easier because you are looking at what other people within the same location are interested in.

Aside from your current location, search engine sites also consider your browsing history. This can again alter your results from another person in the same location that are searching for the same keywords you have typed in. If you want to truly see the page results without other factors altering the results you are going to get, there are a few things that you can do:

1.   Aside from your usual keyword, you can add a location that will make the results more specific towards the location that you are interested in checking out. This is very easy to do and can already give you the result that you want.

2.   Try searching in incognito mode. This will give you an unbiased ranking of the website. It will not be based on how many times you have checked that same website in the past. You will see if the keywords that you have typed in are truly relevant or not.

How to Let Customers Stay at Your Website

Even if you were able to configure your website so that it will be one of the websites that will appear first when people start searching, the ranking would not guarantee that they will continue to navigate your website and actually purchase from you. What do you think should you do in order to let customers stay? You need to work on your website appropriately.

●   Make sure that your website has an appealing design - It will help if the design of your website is something that people find nice to look at. If they think that your website looks dirty and if the different links are all over the place, then it will not be very pleasing.

●   The design that you are going to pick out should be connected to drop shipping - It does not necessarily have to have the word drop shipping all over the website but rather, your website should look like a drop shipping site with a twist.

●   The navigation should be easy - If people do not understand how to get from one page to another, then you can already expect that navigation will not be very easy to do and you will lose potential customers in the process.

- Get rid of ads that cover the whole page - One of the things that can turn off a lot of people into visiting various websites is having an advertisement flashed on the screen. If this is something that you never liked in other websites before then why should you do it to yours?

- Let customers browse through your website before giving them an option to register so that they can start purchasing from your website. Remember that when you force people to register for your website, you can expect that they will rather not go through with it.

- Add videos and images - Do not underestimate the power of videos and images on your website. Each item that you are selling should have images because you want people to see how the items look like. Just be specific if you think that the item may not look exactly the same with how it looks like in pictures. Videos can be endearing for some and can let them stay for more than a few minutes.

- Let them find what they need - You may want to put a lot of fluff, but it would be similar to having a useless PowerPoint presentation with a lot of animation. You do not need to let your website become animated to become noticed. They have checked your website in the first place in order to look at your items. Let them see what items you are selling. It will make a huge difference with how long they will stay.

- Do not have a laggy site - Do you know one of the reasons why people decide to navigate away from a website? It is because the website is not responding properly to the actions that they want. For example, if they click on an item with the use of their mouse button, it takes more than 10 seconds before the image becomes big enough for them to see. When your website is laggy, they would rather search elsewhere.

- If you have links, make sure that they are easy to find - There may be some links that they can click on in order to get to another portion of your website. Make these links visible.

- Have a page on your website that talks about the frequently asked questions regarding your website, what you offer and the things that you sell. Remember that no matter how nice you thought you had created your website, there are some customers who will not understand a few things. As long as you place some FAQ, your customers will know that you are trying your best to address their current issues.

Figuring Out the Rest

At this point in time, you already know how you can compete with competitors so that people will start checking out your website too but how will you know if the strategies that you are planning will actually work? You will never know if it is going to work or not. There are some people who were able to implement changes to their website at the right time, so they become more established easier but there are also some who may have to struggle for months before they become noticed by customers.

Chapter 9 Understand and Figure Out Your Sales Channel

By now, you should have decided what products you want to sell and the suppliers from whom to source them. Your business is now more or less established. Therefore, it is time to get to the most exciting part: selling the products!

Before you do, you have to give a thought to the sales channels you want to use. The sales channel is how you get your products in front of your prospective customers. Now, there are quite a few sales channels available for you to use. However, when you are running a business, you will generally end up using Amazon, eBay, or your very own online store.

Let us take a look at each of the above in turn to get a better understanding.

Using eBay in Your Drop Shipping Business

Most people are familiar with eBay. After all, it is the biggest online auction site in the world for all kinds of physical goods. Due to its huge size, there are various reasons for you to start drop shipping on this site. However, there are also reasons for not doing so.

The advantages of using eBay

Get Started Easily: It is quite easy to start using eBay immediately. It takes a few minutes to create a new account on eBay and a further few minutes to add a listing of your product. You can then start selling the very same day.

Immediate access to an enormous audience: One of the biggest benefits of eBay is that there are millions of people who visit this auction site and make purchases frequently. By using eBay, you will get immediate access to this thriving market full of potential customers. Hundreds of customers will be seeing your listing regularly. Being an active market, you are sure to make sales in a short period of time.

Decreased need for marketing: Since you are using eBay, you do not have to worry much about marketing. You do not need to pay to get traffic or invest in SEO techniques for attracting customers. You can save a considerable investment of time and resources in your business. After all, marketing is always one of the major challenges of launching and running a drop shipping business or any business for that matter.

The disadvantages of using eBay

Fees for Listing: One of the biggest problems with eBay is that you have to pay listing fees. One of these fees is the success fee, which you pay when your item is sold. The success fee can climb as high as 10% of the sale prices and even higher in some cases.

Now, the margins in the drop shipping business are quite low as it is. By paying these fees, you will be decreasing your profits even further. This can be a major hindrance to your earnings.

The Lack of Customizability: While eBay does allow you to customize your product listings a bit, the options are not very extensive. You will have to follow the templates provided. As a result, it is quite difficult to create a professional page that adds value to the listings of your items.

The Lack of Long-Term Customer Connection: When you are selling on eBay, you can attract a few repeat customers. However, most people are not going to buy from you again. Therefore, you are not likely to generate much goodwill by providing excellent services to each individual customer and, even if you do, it will not be of much use. Of course, excellent service is necessary to get good ratings, which can help you get other customers. However, eBay does not give you much leeway in communicating with customers. There are also limits to how you can brand yourself, among other things. This is due to the fact that the marketplace structure in eBay has been designed to be self-serving as eBay focuses on the products and not the merchants.

Need for Constant Monitoring: The marketplace structure in eBay is auction style. Therefore, it is your responsibility to monitor your listings constantly and relist the products when the time runs out. You can certainly use tools to automate the whole process but, even so, the absence of having a static product listing can be a problem.

Not an Asset: You can create your own online store which has repeat customers and generates traffic. Such a store will be a real business that has value. As such, it can be an asset that can be sold to others. When you are selling on eBay, you will not be building a web property or even a brand that possesses value. In other words, it will not be an asset that can be sold to others in the future.

Using Amazon in Your Drop Shipping Business

Amazon is a different ballgame from eBay. Amazon has its own products that it stocks and sells through its online store. At the same time, the majority of the products listed on Amazon are actually sold via Amazon by third party merchants. In this case, Amazon acts a platform and intermediary to make the sale possible. It is also there to resolve any and all problems that can arise. Unlike eBay, there are no auctions on Amazon.

The advantages of using Amazon

Start Easily: As with eBay, it is quite easy to start selling on Amazon. You simply need to register a seller account and create the listings of your product.

Access to Large Audience: Amazon is well-established and it serves millions of customers daily. Therefore, you will be getting access to the considerable audience as soon as you list the products. However, unlike eBay, you need to consider the country in which you would like to sell the products. Generally, you should consider selling products in the same country that your business has been registered in, especially when you are just starting your business.

Lesser Degree of Marketing: Amazon is a widely recognized online store. As such, there is no need to worry about marketing when you are selling on Amazon. There is no need to invest in marketing techniques like SEO for getting customers. After all, the customers are already there on Amazon.

Availability of Fulfillment Warehouses: You should recall Amazon FBA. It is another advantage of using Amazon for your drop shipping business. The great thing is that you can use the FBA warehouses along with your other drop shipping suppliers. As a result, there is no longer any need for shipping, packing, or warehousing.

The disadvantages of using Amazon

Fees for Listing: As with eBay, you are required to pay certain fees in order to use the services provided by Amazon. The commission fees charged by Amazon depend on the type of product you are selling. However, being in the range of 10% to 15%, the fees are rather substantial. If your margins are low, your earnings through drop shipping can be considerably decreased.

Disclosure of Sales Data: One of the things that you should know about Amazon is that your entire sales data is visible to Amazon. In other words, Amazon knows which items are your best sellers and how much you are selling.

Lack of Customer Connection: This is another way in which Amazon is similar to eBay. It can be difficult to develop a good relationship and connection with your customers on Amazon. After all, there are limits to the branding and display of your products. However, it is still easier to make a good customer connection compared to eBay. This is due to the presence of features such as fulfillment by Amazon and Prime, among other things.

Lack of Customization: The lack of customization options is worse on Amazon than eBay. In eBay, you get a template to create your product listing on. In Amazon, you can just place the technical details and the product description for the listing. There is nothing else in terms of branding or UI, among other things, as they are controlled by Amazon.

Using Your Own Online Store in Your Drop Shipping Business

If you do not wish to use existing online marketplaces such as eBay and Amazon, there is another option that you can use, and that is to create your very own online store. With an online store, you can sell your own products. This method is quite popular among people who want to start their drop shipping business success.

The advantages of using your own online store

Greater Control: One of the biggest benefits of using your own online store is that you get complete control over it. You can create an environment that is conducive to the sale of your products and items. At the same time, these stores can add value to the people looking to shop for you. You can customize the online store and make your own layout and appearance. You can also do wonderful stuff, such as custom pages for each product. In short, you can optimize your online store to increase the sale of your products.

Ease of Design: You do not have to worry about your ecommerce store. It has become quite easy to make your own ecommerce store these days, thanks to platforms such as Shopify. With the tools they offer, you can make a custom design for your online store quite easily. You can select a store design out of the templates provided and make the customizations necessary. Finally, you can add the products, implement a payment gateway and your online store is ready for business. In fact, you can do all of this in just one day.

Avoid Third-Party Fees: This is another beneficial aspect of using your own store. There is no need to pay any commission fees, as you are not using the services provided by someone else. This can improve your earnings and profit margins by a considerable margin. In fact, it is possible to earn more with your own store than it is by using services like eBay and Amazon.

Mobile-Readiness: In order to enjoy this benefit, you need to use a good ecommerce platform to create your online store. You have to make sure that your store has a responsive design that looks good on mobile devices like smart phones and tablets. This can help increase your sales, as a significant percentage of online sales take place through mobile devices. Additionally, some platforms allow you to manage your online store through your mobile device. Therefore, you can take a vacation without worrying about your business as you can take it with you in your pocket.

Building an Asset: With an online store, you gain the ability to build up a real business that has its own feel and branding. It will have repeat customers and known expertise in its niche. In other words, it will be an asset with equity. Therefore, you can sell this business entity in the future if you want.

The disadvantages of using your own online store

Greater Complexity: When you are using services like eBay and Amazon, you do not have to think a lot when you are creating listings. You simply need to fill up the template provided and get your listings published. This is not the case with your own site. While you get more customization options, it also becomes your responsibility to use those options. You have to determine the structure and design of the store, among other things. If you are going to host your online store on your own, then you will also have to consider the technical details of the servers and software, etc. Therefore, running an online store is more complicated.

Marketing Investment: Since it is your own site, it also becomes your responsibility to ensure that it is getting a steady flow of customers. As a result, you will have to start thinking about SEO, paid advertising, and other marketing techniques. You will have to invest money as well as time in the development of a long-term campaign for the promotion of your online store. This will allow you to get the customers you need to make your store a profitable enterprise.

Chapter 10 Minimize Expenses to Increase Profit

You can decrease your costs and increase your profits by doing the following:

Minimizing Costs

To minimize the cost of operating your dropshipping venture, implement the following steps:

Use Free Options Whenever they Are Available: While starting a business, your aim should be to minimize startup costs as much as you can. To do that, use free options instead of paid ones. For example, as you search for suppliers, start with using Google and only move to directories once the business starts paying for itself. Using this technique, you can save the extra $50 you would have used to pay for directories. Use this amount on advertising to get better results.

First Target Local Market: As you get started, instead of targeting the international markets, target your local market so you can save on expensive international shipping costs. Once your business starts going well, dive into international markets.

Buy Hosting Plans for 3 or 6 months: When creating a website for your business, instead of buying a full year hosting plan that can cost you $100, choose a 3 or 6-month plan. This helps you save some money in the short run, which is necessary because you are yet to know whether your business is going to work. You can get 3 months hosting for only $35–40, which can save you $60–65 if your business fails to succeed.

Sell Small in Size Goods: As mentioned earlier in this book, this can save you shipping costs. Once your business succeeds, you can introduce large sized goods as well.

Maximizing Profits

1: Sell On Amazon & eBay

The best way to increase your sales and profits is by creating accounts on reputable sites such as Amazon and eBay. You can leverage on the reputation and traffic that these websites enjoy in order to grow your revenues and customer base. The fact that people (customers) trust the Amazon, eBay or Etsy brand will make it easy for you to get orders, probably drive traffic to your website and ultimately grow your brand as well.

2: Upsell

Additionally, you should have in place an up selling strategy since up selling is the best way to increase sales. Once a customer adds a product to his or her shopping cart, offer another product that complements the product the customer choses at a discounted price. This will definitely increase your number of product sales and hence your profit margins. Don't forget to use that strategy even when listing on some reputable ecommerce stores.

For instance, if a customer visits your e-store and adds a pair of earrings to her shopping cart, offer that customer a jewelry box that compliments those earrings at a discounted price. The chances of the customer buying a jewelry box and the earrings are higher when compared to the customer buying the jewelry box alone.

3: Offer variety

Additionally, deal in more than one category. The more products you have, the better your chances of acquiring more customers: do not stick to just one niche. For example, if you are dealing in women clothes, you can add more categories of products such as women shoes, jewelry, bags, etc.

Implement all the strategies mentioned in this book and soon enough, you will have on your hands a profitable drop shipping business.

Chapter 11 Automating Your Store

How to automate your store. I work on some of my stores only two hours a week because I've automated it all. Yes, you heard me, two hours. Screw your four-hour work week! Most of that is just managing payments or a supplier asking me a question etc.

Now since I've named five methods in this book, you'll need to make sure that you use the correct method for each one of these types of drop shipping. A lot of this requires trust because you're relying on software and virtual assistants.

I've got all the software and websites for virtual assistants in the PDF to make it easy for you.

Now for the methods of:

• eBay – Amazon

• Print on Demand

• Retail Arbitrage

• Aliexpress

• Supplier

eBay – Amazon:

For the eBay – Amazon method, since this method is pretty much relying on eBay traffic which is huge which means you don't need to pay for advertising. You're basically in a pricing war with everyone else.

This method is pretty much autopilot because since you're only using two platforms, there's plenty of software out there willing to help you. Only using two platforms reduces complications thus making software easy.

My favorite is Profit Scraper. This piece of magical software manages to do this type of dropshipping from A to Z. It will list products for you from Amazon to eBay in just a few clicks and also auto-order products from Amazon to your customer on eBay. I don't think I've seen such an all in one software like this before and this should be taken advantage of.

I'm not going to lie, this isn't a free piece of software however they do allow you to have 7 days free as a trial to see whether you like it or not. However, if you're going to be making money off something always expect someone else trying to make a buck whilst you're making a buck too to make your life easier. Just appreciate it. This software makes it completely auto-pilot once you've got your products listed. It even has an auto price which makes it definitely passive.

Again, the link to this software is on the PDF.

Retail Arbitrage:

For retail arbitrage using either an eBay store or a Shopify store, there really only is one method and that's using a virtual assistant or even a few to start off with. I first of all started off with 5 because money loves speed so I decided to get 5 on the go so they can list as many products as possible. As I've got a Shopify store, I basically got 500 products on my store within 3 days because all of it is just copy and pasting products from your niche.

Once you've got a good amount of products on your website and that it also makes your website look like it was for a specific niche and not just a general store then you can expect customers to come in once you've got your advertising sorted.

With Shopify there are staff accounts where you can let one of your virtual assistants use so they can access the orders for that day. You will then give them your credit card number, yes this is a step up, you need to have trust and preferably a credit card made specifically for them such as a top up prepaid card. They will then use the orders and that card to purchase the products for the customer.

A lot of times, since a lot of virtual assistants don't know this method, they'll need training. You'll use a screen capture software such as screen-cast-o-matic to show them what they have to do such as listing and buying from vendors using their cards. If they've already had training before by someone else then you're in luck!

These virtual assistants usually cost $3-5 per hour or you can just pay a fixed price for certain tasks such as paying $100 for 250 listed products. I recommend when doing your business to use virtual assistants from the Philippines because although you might be paying peanuts, their minimum wage is around the $1.5 mark so you're doing well for them. Philippines also adopts similar education to us in English countries so a lot of the time, you'll find that they are very fluent in English.

They can also manage your customer service however a lot of them won't be perfect English so if you allow them to do it, you may not get return customers because they may think you're not an American/English company. They also are in a different time zone so when your customers are asking questions, they won't be awake to respond to them.

I recommend either getting your customer service outsourced by an actual customer service company such as support ninja.

Finally to find these virtual assistants, you'll have to use a freelance website such as UpWork. All you have to do is post a job about doing certain tasks then people looking for work will come flocking to you. After posting you've got to interview those for English skills and competency then hire them if you feel they are worth it. Sometimes they might be more expensive than Bangladeshi or Pakistani virtual assistants however it's definitely worth it with their better English skills.

Print on Demand:

For print on demand, you'll start off either creating your own designs or hiring someone to do the designs for you. I always hire because my creativity literally doesn't exist. But I'd usually bulk buy a ton of designs such as 100 and then pay less because of the bulk order. I usually pay $5 per design depending on the quantity I want to buy. You will then upload them up to your store and advertise the shirts as you would.

With apps such as Printful for Shopify, as soon as you get an order for your shirt, the app will automatically process the order and fulfill it for you. All you have to do is list and upload the information to Printful. They will bill you for each shirt obviously but when you get orders, you don't have to go on their website to order because the app will have already done that. Printful is also another print on demand dropshipper with excellent Shopify integration.

Aliexpress:

For Aliexpress when using a Shopify store, there's many options however there's one that everyone uses. This one option just makes the whole process extremely smooth and to be honest, it can make the store side of your business fully automated and really all you've got to do is monitor and do your Facebook ads. If you're willing to pay someone on UpWork who is experienced on Facebook ads then you've got the whole process outsourced completely, however hiring experienced marketers can be very experienced because learning it is very expensive with lots of trial and error and the actual skill itself takes a lot of monitoring and all that jazz.

Once you find your niche, you can start putting products onto your shore and this is where the Shopify app called "Oberlo" is going to come into play. It's something similar to profit scraper in the fact that it will import products from Aliexpress into your store on Shopify and will also order the product once a customer has bought it.

I really love this software, it's relatively new of the time of writing however it's definitely still brilliant for how young it is and I'm pretty sure it's going to be a piece of software worth over $50 million sooner or later.

Whenever you're going through Aliexpress, you'll find yourself needing to enter into each individual product page looking for the ePacket option which is very long and frustrating sometimes. Oberlo shows you what products have this already as an option to save you lots of time.

It also changes your prices when your supplier prices change, remember the suppliers are entrepreneurs too and not slaves so don't be expecting them to be on the rock bottom of prices. So having something else monitor the pricing for you is very good.

Also to compliment the price checker, it also has a stock checker. For whenever you are selling an item and it runs out of stock, the app will take care of it and not list that product no more until stock is available again.

Finally it fulfills the orders for you. Whenever a product is ordered by your customer, Oberlo will take you to a proceed page where you'll have to just click a few times with no keyboard typing. You just watch it do its thing, whenever the supplier fulfills the order and gives the ePacket tracking code, Oberlo also provides that to your customer whenever it's available.

This software isn't even very expensive thankfully. It's $14.90 for 50 orders and 500 orders for $29.99, this considering the amount of time and profit you'll be making is pretty decent. If you're spending a good amount for advertising you'll find yourself reaching to the $29.99 pretty quickly however if you're starting off, just go for the $14.90, oh yeah, it also has a trial period for whether you like it or not.

The one thing I should warn you about this software is whenever you're importing products that you should be wary about the English used by the supplier. Since these suppliers the majority of the time aren't natively English, they can sometimes screw up in the title or product description or whatever so make sure to double check their grammar and spelling. As mentioned in the Shopify chapter, having bad English can really turn a customer off so be wary.

Supplier:

Now this is similar to retail arbitrage however since you're allowed to do this sort of dropshipping on Amazon, Shopify and eBay, we'll go through all of them.

With Amazon, you don't have to spend much money if at all like eBay on advertising and marketing but your margins might be smaller because of the competitiveness and fees. However, ignoring that, you'll not need to spend money straight away if you're going to do everything yourself.

With supplier in general, you're going to need to use virtual assistants because there's no software out there that allows you to do all the stores plus your own store.

Amazon has an account system where you the admin of the Amazon account/company will have control of everything. Then you can get sub accounts to your main account that will allow you to direct tasks to specific virtual assistants. These sub accounts allow you to block certain permissions such as looking at orders but only listing products.

You have to go on UpWork and find an assistant who can do this for you and if they can't then you can train them. It's not very difficult however make sure to fire quick if they're doing things wrong and don't try to give into sympathy because you're only going to be hurting yourself. This is one of the main mistakes that why many startup businesses fail because they usually give too much capital away for second chances when there's already ready-made talent out there. If you're going to be taking anything away from this book, you should take away the fact that you have to fire quick.

Again I recommend that you to use a prepaid card to give to your VA if you plan on letting them order products from the supplier.

Though with a lot of suppliers they will allow you to collect orders through the day and then email them a spreadsheet of products you need to be delivered on that day and their deadline is usually 3pm. This allows the supplier to have the dispatched by the time they have a delivery van waiting for them on the same day. However from my experience, a lot of suppliers just prefer me to do an order as we go on instead of bulking up near the end of the day.

Chapter 12 Conclusion

Dropshipping can provide the opportunity for those who have little financial means to start their own business and with hard work can provide a reasonable income. However, it should never be confused with a get rich quick scheme. To be a successful dropshipper you will need to adopt a professional, business approach to your project. You must devise a plan and decide on a goal; it can often help to split your main goal down into a series of mini-goals which are achievable every week or month. This is important as it will help you to realise you are becoming successful. Alternatively, if you are not where you expect to be you can consider your position and the options in comparison to your plan and how the business is currently working. You can also adjust your plan accordingly.

Dropshipping is a competitive business model and it can be difficult to pick the right products and market sector without encountering heavy competition from established businesses. If this is the case and you do not wish to change your product or strategy then you must consider the best approach. There will always be something you can offer customers that the current market leader cannot. In fact it is possible to learn a huge amount from an established company; which sites it is active on and what marketing tactics it uses. You can study the competition and learn these items; this is likely to give you an idea as to how you can offer something that adds value from the customer's point of view. The more value they believe they are getting the more likely they will be to purchase an item from you rather than from their original supplier.

Dropshipping offers a reduced risk method of starting your own business but it also offers very small profit margins; to be successful with a dropshipping business by itself you will need either a large number of customers for each product or a large number of products with a few people eager to buy each item. It is easy to generate additional interest through social media and other marketing methods than it is to promote a larger range of products. It is also worth noting that traditional marketing and business techniques will work just as well with a dropshipping business.

This book has been designed to help you understand what is involved in being a dropshipper and how it is a business which is open to anyone. The key to being successful is in the way you deal with other people and the customer service you provide; it is this that will differentiate you from the other dropshipping business offering the same products.

It is important to note that when you are searching for a dropshipping supplier you may come across several scams. People finding their feet in this industry are relatively easy prey and can be parted from their money easily if they have not completed their research. Anyone dropshipping supplier who wants payment up front should be walked away from; they may be genuine but it is highly unlikely; they are more likely to be after your money! For every genuine business opportunity there will probably be someone trying to get funds from you. However, as you should by now know, the start up cost of dropshipping is minimal; they consist of web hosting, domain registration and possibly a payment receiving package. All stock should be paid for at the time you order it; which is when the customer orders it from you.

The best way to ensure you are successful is to keep the lines of communication open at all times; build a relationship with your customers and stay in regular contact. Your customer contact should remind them of who you are and what you can offer them of value; this will ensure you remain in their thoughts when they need a product that you may sell. You also need to keep a good level of communication with your suppliers; the better the relationship you have the easier it will be to resolve any issues with supply problems or missing stock. You may also find that if you have a good relationship with your supplier you can get access to special offers, discounts or simply stock when there is a limited amount left.

This book should have inspired you to believe it is possible to start your own business and become a successful dropshipper. Despite the level of competition there are niches available which can still provide a profitable return; study your chosen niche and ensure you know which products will sell and which sector of the market you need to target. Dropshipping may not expose you to the risks that other start-ups can but it can still fail and cost you more money than you expect or even than you have made.

Top Drop Shipping Items to Sell

Drop shipping is a really easy to set up and convenient business, but you must always consider some elements of the business before you begin. You must be aware that all products don't sell equally with online retailing. Sometimes, it's not even practical for a particular type of product to be drop shipped. To help you decide some of the products you could start out with, here is a list of a few products which are really popular and sell better using drop shipping methods.

Computer Accessories

This age is called the machine age, and quite aptly so. People are always upgrading their computers with new hardware parts, and for this reason, computer accessories are really popular. Drop shippers can make good money out of selling computer accessories as they are relatively easy to ship and aren't too bulky or perishable. You can provide people with special schemes and offers to convince them into buying multiple products at once, so all the parts can be shipped to them together. This makes things easier for both the supplier and the customer. According to various surveys, computer parts are one of the top selling products for drop shipping businesses.

Beauty Products

Beauty products are something people need all the time. They are not one-time-buy products. So you can be pretty sure that if the customer who once bought from you is satisfied with the delivery speed and buying experience, then he or she will return and buy it from you again. These items run out quick and customers buy them frequently. These are the items with which you can create brand loyalty and goodwill. Develop strong positive relationships with buyers so they come back and buy from you again.

Clothing

If you can be sure of one thing that shall always stay in demand, it's clothes. This steady demand for clothing is what makes it such a great product for drop shipping. If buyers are satisfied with one dress they bought from you, they will come back to buy a whole wardrobe from you. Children grow up and need new clothes every year or every few months, so make sure you provide people with a good buying experience. It will work in your favor. Drop shipping is also great for this item because you don't have to handle the clothes yourself. You can mooch off the already earned brand image of other big brands.

Fashion Accessories

Fashion accessories are just like clothing in their demand. They are always high in demand, and this gives you - the seller - an advantage. Accessories are always changing, new ones coming in and out of trend as seasons change and years pass. People need sunglasses in summer and hats in winter. Something that is fashionable to wear right now might be completely out of trend by this time next year. The great thing about selling accessories via drop shipping is that you don't have to keep any stock, hence excluding any risk of overstocking and it becoming obsolete. You don't handle any of the products yourself, so you can pay all your attention to sales and marketing strategies.

Mobile Phones

There are always new and improved mobile phones hitting the market, every day, every month. The competition is tough, and the manufacturers know it. They are always working on newer and better models. Similarly, customers want to stay ahead of others and wait for new models excitedly. This works in your favor as a drop shipping seller because you can offer the buyer a lot of variety, which he or she might not get in a single brand store. You don't have to convince anyone into buying anything. You can just display the features on your website, and it is for the customer to choose.

Tickets

Getting tickets for anything can be a cumbersome experience. One has to wait in queues for long durations at times, and everyone dislikes that. Drop shipping tickets to buyers allows buyers to make last minute purchases and avoid the hassle of waiting in queues.

Books

Books are hands down the most popular and in demand product according to most surveys. Buyers often spend hours browsing in this section, and people of all ages like to read. You can use drop shipping to provide books at cheaper costs to the buyers while using multiple publishers.

Toys

Power Home Biz calls toys another really popular category for customers. Toys are suitable for drop shipping. Children easily get bored with their current toys, and convince parents into buying them new ones. Toys are both entertaining and educating, and hence are bought fairly often, bringing frequent business for you.

Furniture

Furniture is needed by almost everyone who has a house. And it happens to be bulky and heavy and just very non-cooperating in general, which sucks. Drop shipping comes to your rescue and ensures your customers get their furniture on time and in perfect condition, all of it without you having to even see or touch the furniture, let alone handle it. You save on massive transportation costs, and it also eliminates the need for you to pay various customs and duties. Furniture is, thus, a popular product for drop shipping.

Media

You can also sell music, video games, and movies with the help of drop shipping. They are really popular, and with the constant influx of new media in the market all the time, you can be pretty optimistic the purchases will never stop if the customers enjoy a good buying experience.

Reference:

ADDISON, G. (2017). *DROPSHIPPING*. [S.l.]: LULU COM.

Neil, J. (2016) *Dropshipping 101*.

Youderian, A. (2016) *The ultimate guide to dropshipping*.

www.ingramcontent.com/pod-product-compliance
Lightning Source LLC
Chambersburg PA
CBHW051336220526
45468CB00004B/1674